I AM THE HIDDEN TRACK ON YOUR MOON PLAYLIST

play this 3 AM song

Melanie Soyah

VOLUME 1

Copyright © 2021 Melanie Soyah

Autor: Melanie Soyah
Umschlaggestaltung, Illustration: Melanie Soyah
Übersetzung: Melanie Soyah

Verlag & Druck: tredition GmbH, Halenreie 40-44, 22359 Hamburg
ISBN:
978-3-347-32900-3 (Paperback)
978-3-347-32901-0 (Hardcover)
978-3-347-32902-7 (e-Book)

Bibliografische Information der Deutschen Nationalbibliothek:
Die Deutsche Nationalbibliothek
verzeichnet diese Publikation
in der Deutschen Nationalbibliografie; detaillierte
bibliografische Daten sind im Internet über http://dnb.d-nb.de
abrufbar.

Melanie is probably one of the most gifted
and still humble persons I know.
All she does and all she is, is love, laughter and heartwarming
presence.
Not to completely fall in love with her right away is impossible.

— *loving, mourning, freeing!*

One gets sucked into the cosmos of devastation and longing from
the very first second. Not only the words are art but poems
themselves are presented; sometimes broken and torn, sometimes
overly present, sometimes depicting vulnerability and most of the
times unconditonal strength and love. At the end you are desperate
to know if the person addressed heard the message or if the author
was left heart-broken.'

Cava

I am not the same having
seen the moon shine on
the other side of the
world"

-Rademacher

This

display

speaks no longer

00:00

01:13

02:00

02:33

02:55

03:00

03:17

04:25

04:44

04:56

no sleep

Welcome

to

my

3 AM

song

Star by Star

One is for you, two is for me, three is SHE, four
is just to see you better, five is just
to read you better, s i x is to feel you better,
seven is to breath better with you, so, eight is
more for keeping you safe, nine is for our
floating in this atmosphere
ten is just for her.

So, let one star be for low pain
and the other one
for you and me in the rain,
the next one is
for more faith in this
and that one for just a lifetime
K i S S
one is for the love you choose
the next one for YOU
I will never lose
the other one is for holding your hand and the
next one for less weight on our land
and this one for more and more shine out of your
eyes
so, what's left to say the last one whispers "I
love you, without any whys"

Ultimately

Y O U

Enter

My

Piece

Of

Paper

Firstshe
wanted
to
fly
to
the
moon
withme
butthen
withthetime
the
moon
gotsovery
boredofus
thathe
fell
from
the
sky

may

your

silence

be

audible

inthecalm

&

maytheglowofthemoon

keepyoursecret

until

your

love

finds

me

                                    YOU THINK
                                  YOU ARE THE
                      CENTER OF THE UNIVERSE
                                  BUT YOU GET
                                     LOST IN
                          YOUR OWN LABYRINTH

                                       -

this
is
how
it
goes:
I
feel
your
worries
pouring
out of your
skin

Oh, lie

oh,

how good you are

you cloud my mind

and I don't realize

how awful

the truth is

which is me

CAN YOU GIVE ME THE PASSWORD TO YOUR HEART?

and then by

3AM

I went to my sofa

I turned

it ǝpᴉsdn down

I

shook it

like a pillow

just to see

how you

fall out. . .

2 3:4 5 PM
What song are you listening to?
Can I dive
into this beat?

Her eyes pierce

my body

cut tears in my skin

her nose is stuck

in my secrets

pulls my

stomache tight

her mouth forms

beautiful words

threateningly

close

(she said: this was me)

S.11

I f

I

h i t

t h e

m o o n

w h a t

w o u l d

b e

n e x t?

MY

HEART

IS

AN

EMPTY ROOM

MY

WALLS

IN

DEEPEST BLUE

BUT

I AM

TALKING

LIKE

MAD

RED

TO YOU

Sitting
Right
Here
The
Pen
On
ME
just
Waiting
To
Start
The
Fight

What

is a better way

to prop up

a

fading

heart

than

to start

a

war?

EVERYTHING
IS
TIGHTER
THAN
SKIN
CAN`T
YOU
SEE
THE
WAY
WE
ARE
MOVING
IN

A

Wandering

scar—

Just

Another

Cut !

WHY
DID
YOU
LEAVE
ME
UNDER
THE
MOON
WITH
A
PACK
OF
WOLVES?

and
I break your heart
in two
one for me
and
one for . . .

You are not here

And if you were here

I wouldn't be able to write this

LOST

IN

THE

HEAD

OF

YOU!

Right here

I

AM

throwing away my clothes

they are too worn

Right here

I

AM

throwing a heart

which I have shared with many people

Right here

I

AM

throwing

your name

into the direction of the moon

you are too worn

let go

let go of me

you are not quite your look

then take it away

you are

an alibi

you are

not final

you are

my unwritten book

You stay but i will go

SPARE

ME

YOUR

LOVE

TEAR

MY

HEART

OUT

OF YOUR

CHEST

I cry without tears every
night
I miss you:
even if it makes me even
more lonely
I would rather die that way
and prefer not to speak!
And I will no longer ask
what makes sense

She hated what she did

not understand.

And she did not

understand.

~~Off~~
Into the world
Into the stars
Into the ocean
Into the moon
Not longer into you
You can wait!

Every touch from you makes
me untouchable for others
and reminds me of
the million times
I will be loved,
but not from you

1:07 4:37

a n d

I

s w i p e

y o u r

f a c e

a n d

s w i p e s w i p e y o u a w a y

v e r y

s l o w l y s l o w l y s l o w l y

5.30

Nobody has hurt

her so deeply

and she never stopped planning to get even. She

has shredded the most beautiful in the name of

love.

Now she wants the strongest on

to **BREAK** it!

.

we create memories

we broke all our promises

```
                    THIS
                     ME
                    AND
               WHAT IS THIS
                     ME
                  WITHOUT
                    ME?
              ALIENATED MIND
              ALIENATED SOUL
               FROM NOW ON
               EVERYBODY IS
                   ONLY
                    AN
                  OBJECT
```

I am a witness of you and me

even if you deny it

even if you wipe it out

I held your heavy head

I warmed your cold heart

I kissed your lying tongue

I bit your scared skin

and all the other shit where you

had pushed me in

I
W
A
N
T
T
O
F
U
C
K

A
W
A
Y
M
Y
F
E
A
R

I have got a

3 AM

o

v

e

r

d

o

s

e

This kiss
I never gave
you can't forgive
me!!!
It
just doesn't give
up and makes
living very
difficult for me
as
much
as
possible
it
tickles
my
lips
and
pushes through my
ribs
it makes noises in my soul
slit in my throat
and dashes through the brain!!!

I think

I   just

swallowed   a

star!

(itwasyourfaceisaw)

What

a
fool

I am

that

I

seemed

to

believe

my

imperfection

could be the fault

How

many drinks, drinks, drinks

do you

need till

you miss

me?

My mouth
is taped shut
from now
on.
My hands
are stuck on
the <u>keyboard...</u>

if my words could
choose a good ending
I would hug them
all night long
until the pain is over

I want nothing

I am not looking for anything

I will take my time

1 0 0 0

Errors

D A M N,

IT WAS YOUR

HEAD

WITH

1 0 0 0

Errors

UNTIL

I

NOTICED

THAT

YOUR

1 0 0 0

Errors

BECAME

MY

1 0 0 0

Errors

O n t h e
f o l l o w i n g
p a g e
i
w i l l
w r i t e
y o u r
n a m e
back and forth
p r o b a b l y 5 0 0 t i m e s
but no one really cares

. . .

In hate

I

wanted you most:

Deeper look

to the point of

annoyance,

a tense laugh

and while I held your hand

I noticed

you are already gone.

It hurts not to be able to

say how much

I regret everything!

you way too big

you this thing

you too shiny

you got those eyes

You too much

-not a single moment of me

and who I usually want to be

you got this runaway thing

you too down

you got blue endlessness

A n y w a y

you too dark

you got the night on your back

(I am the night)

you way too black

you too soft

you got this skin

your line my line (thin line)

you got this heart

can a I have it for a while

I will squeeze and press it till your heart gives

me back that thankful

s m i l e

B u t y o u w a y too much

you

your d e m o n s f u c k the truth

I

hate

every song

you

sing

Let the sky wipe you away
Let the moon bleed on you
Let the stars cut your face
Nothing should spear you
You love the brutality
Here you go
You are just a scream, pain and sweat
PERiOD

YOU ARE MY STAR
UNFORTUNATELY
STARS ARE GLOWING STONES
AND STONES ARE CRUEL
AND DEAD
AND WITHOUT SHINE

SUDDENLY THERE IS YOU

I DON'T WANT YOU TO BE HERE

M I S S I N G

P U N C T U A T I O N

BUT WITH A LOT OF DEEP SIGHS

There
Came
No
Fucking
Word
For
Over
200
Days
You
Have
To
Fucking
Speak
At
Last

`YOU ARE DOING WELL`

HARD TO BELIEVE.

THE SUN SHINES.

IT CAN'T GET

Colder

What I had

what she didn't want
what she couldn't want

because it was foreign to her-

so, I took everything I had
and also took what I never had

and never gave it back to her

1. Delete chat
   history
2. Delete photos
3. Delete number
4. Erase
   memories
5. If this all does
   not work
6. ?

even my breath will

overcome the storm

it's just like that:

you had no other choice

you just want to live

but why:

`off all people I had to get

y o u

as an

e n e m y`

THUNDER

THUNDER

THUNDER

Please,

Cut this

3 AM

Time in 2 pieces

Cut my name in two

Cut her heart in two

Please, please, please
be quiet and listen to my
complaints!
    "You are the victim of my

        lines"

My anger for you makes the sea freeze over.

Within

I hit the sand,

until everything

dissolves into each other

Fuck

I am the best

     You are invisible

I am your mirror image

     You are a fucking ice block

I am your melting tear

     You are the darkest night sky

I am your green polar light

     You are the ocean

I am your swallowing fucking wave

     You think you are better than me-
     (but you forget just one single thing)

I am the best

     I am the best

          I am the best

Moon

Companion

this night

call the

stars

shower

with bright glow

my love

far, far

away

I met you as ORCA

YOU became a MONSTER

My

Life

Feels

like

a

Peaceofpaper

Withyou

Completetly

Covered

~~Three AM~~ and forty nine minutes later,
I try to delete the ~~tree AM~~ time now

                                   Far, very far
                        away and I know it will
                             take even longer
                                   2 months
                                  half a year
                                     a year
                                  but she will
                                  return.
                                  Then I should
                                  break her
                                        first
                                  and leave her
                                  for all that
                                  and just walk
                                  away

A Recipe for leaving you:

- Take a bit of your hate
- A dip of your jealousy
- A lot of your true sadness
- A hand full of your helplessness
- Take your broken wings
- And much more of your boring
  lovesongs
- Wait for 5 minutes
Now, mix and shake till you crack
- Wait a moment

- Leave

WHO BREATHES
YOUR BREATH TONIGHT?
THEN WHO WILL
SOON
FEEL WITHOUT YOU
JUST LIKE ME?
COMPLETE

ABANDONED !

You want to give me
New York
But all I want is
Brooklyn

Unfortunately
there is no other compromise
I have no chance against my will.
I am way too scared having to exist without you

Just because

Accidentally maybe

She will burn a hole in my heart

_my heart was
eaten by you

TO FORGET THE

HUMILIATION

OF IMPERFECTION

(would be the best move of my life)

To
breathe
means
to
accept
the
LEAK
intheair

I am
still
trying
to
find
a
way
to
exhale
here...

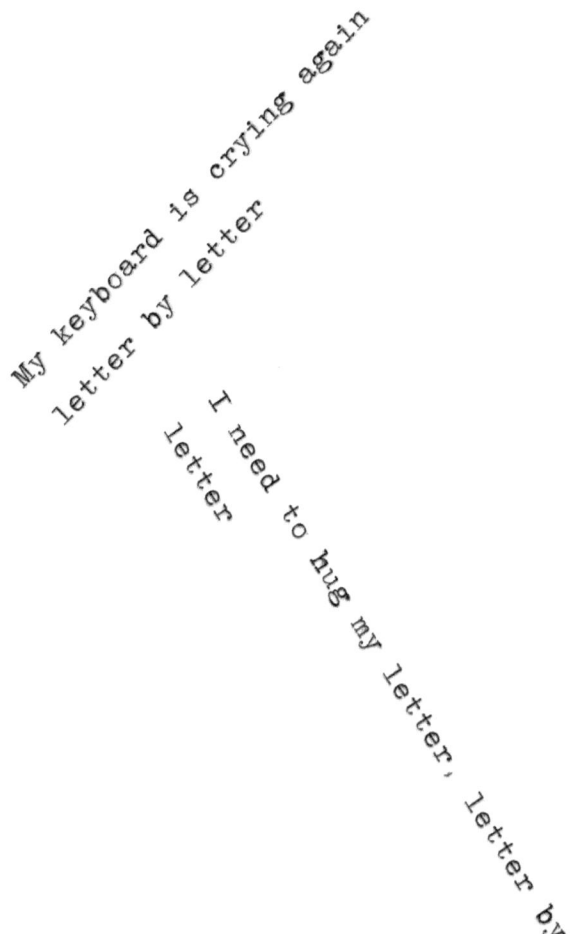

My keyboard is crying again
letter by letter

I need to hug my letter, letter by
letter

no

no

no

it's not LOST without you

it's LOST with you

The universe I saw in you is

c

o

l   l

a

d

s

e

d

S.76

Suddenly
You walked out of me
I feel the shine coming back to
me

You **burned** a hole in my wall

You have been here for

e i g h t h u n d r e d t w e n t y o n e d a y s

A room is not an organ,

lucky me

You wanted to leave me
the last time
but you've come back
a
hundred times
I took you back
a
hundred times
and you took me back
a
million times
and then you dared to give me the
feeling
I am the problem-
finally I will leave you now
the
first time
and
I make this action your problem

No

b u b b l e s

as she

siNKs sAnk

suNK

I am trying to make
something   with   a
phrase   and   a
sentence

no

b o m b

can

achieve

Y o u h a v e n o i d e a h o w
h a r d i d i e w h e n y o u l e f t

I am your indifference
        and my nameless desire dissolves into
                                thin air

Certainly,
I choose this pen
to write a few lines:
How should I look up to the sky
without seeing you
in the moon?
How should I listen to this song
it's not you that's
singing it?
This song so beautifully blue!
How should I sit on my parade
when this person to my left
isn't you on my right?
Now tell me how should
I end my kick
when I know you won't say a single bit?!

I

w a s h

a l l

m y

m e m o r i e s

a w a y

Why did you show me the moon?
Why did you run in those sunsets?
Why did you drink this ocean blue?
Why did you eat the nature green?
Why did you leave so easily
Why did you leave me here on this planet yellow
white?
Why must I stay?
Why can I not go away?

Thoroughly and thoughtless

and without

d e v o t i o n

my brain

cells swim

unconditionally up and

down in my head

and they fight against

the

thought of missing you

but always when the
moon rises
at night
but always when loneliness
chases me in the night
I chase life
with maddening power
hunting alone in the moonlight
I find myself
awakening cold in
the morning after a short dark
night

and I don`t know what I did in this fight

i weep i weep i weep

.

IF
I
WHERE
THE
MOON
SO
YOU
WOULD
BE
HIS
SHINE
TO
BE
CONNECTED
WITH
YOU
FOR
EVER

Finally
This
Was
My
Last
Tear
For
You
It
Was
The
Longest
Night
Of
My
Life
And
It's
Still
Dark
Outside

A single word from you
my soul shatters!

Ah, a new **SONG?**

Hmm,
that sounds like the old one!

I need a place to visit
to
remember
her

CanIstreamyourvoiceon
Spotify

I will not stop

writing this book!

~~You will not read it.~~

But if we last and are not destroyed

and we are durable because

we have lasted.

We do not break easily.

Because we will read it all.

No,

this is not a good ending.

Not the end we had hoped for.

>Not as we thought it

>would be special

>in the long nights

>on the bridge.

Not as we thought

it should be!

I SAW

THE

BEST

VERSION OF

MYSELF

WRITTEN ON

HERSELF

My heart knocks at
my phone!
May I come in?   (I
                    hesitated)

I bring your heart
back that was gone!

They are all not even half of you

They are all not even half of you

They are all not even half of you

They are all not even half of you

They are all not even half of you

They are all not even half of you

They are all not even half of you

They are all not even half of you

They are all not even half of you

They are all not even half of you

They are all not even half of you

They are all not even half of you

Laugh

about the moon

Laugh

about my

3AM

weakness

Laugh

about the sunset

Laugh

about the stars

Laugh

about my words

Laugh

about my s h I n e

even at

3AM

I don't care about

you anymore

3AM

You are gone (you are)

I am here (you are not)

The AM is cut by you (no it was me)

Call me a liar (you are too)

Call me higher (than all the fuckers outside, and
then you)

Call me a million dollar (no you are not)

Call me desire (yours)

                            (forever)

wow

wow

wow

go

go

go

leave, leave, leave

kiss, kiss, kiss

this, this, this

hit me harder

kiss me harder

feel like shit

shit, shit, shit

yay this is your

last hit.

now

now

now

I leave like never before

then by day 1

it takes everything not

to run to you

T h i s pen
has got my number
the number that you keep
there is just one color
to set in motion
again and again, I try to replace it
its features fucked my body deeply
everywhere I turn to face it
but I still chase it
in the same sea of emotions
I blue ink my hand and touch the tide
and expect to feel the ocean
and then
t h i s pen
could rip
the sky open wide
to find your face once again

You pushed me in this cast
Way too fast!
You gave me the **p o w e r**
to part your *h e a r t!*
So, that's how I did it
One part now rises
e a s t
The other part sets in
w e s t!
And which one of us is now,
the b e s t?

THE GRAS IS GREENER WHERE YOU LAY

Y o u a r e t h e o n l y
            p e r s o n
                      I k n o w
            w h o w a n t s
         t o c a r r y
      t h e s t a r s
   o n s m a l l
r a i n d r o p s

So,

I read the past:
how foolish can
someone be?

I
needyouto
write
this
last
line . . .

Can you hold my hand my soul my dream my darkness my
monster my passion my pain my laughter my name my hand
again and again my wings my bones my song my ignorance
my fault my hair my borders my soberness my foot my
body my sickness my pride my ego my shine my sun my
moon my stars my books my words the big me my darkness
my black my white my purple my fingers cross your hair!
Can you hold my invisible heart?
Let's make this visible.
I want to hold your hand feel your soul want to be part
of your dreams want to steel your darkness kill this
monster feed your passion be part of your pain want to
be your laughter your name your hands again and again
your wings to fly your bones to break I want to be your
love song give me your ignorance kill your faults kiss
my hair cross this borders no more soberness (because
of me) I want your foot there between mine hold your
body heal your sickness can I be your pride and your
damn soft ego I want to be your light your sun your
moon and energy I want to be any single star in the
atmosphere I want to be your book every single word
would be about me I turn you into a bigger you I turn
myself into a bigger me I want your darkness your black
and your white and become purple because of me that's
now everything I see.

Good Night **M.Soyah**

THANK YOU
TIME AND SPACE FOR GIVING ME THIS OPPORTUNITY.

THANK YOU
B

I want to say a special
thank you to
Cava

This song
isn't you!
This song
is mine!

MELANIE SOYAH

I AM THE HIDDEN TRACK ON YOUR MOON PLAYLIST

YOU WILL
NEVER KILL
MY VIBE

VOLUME 2

. . . no, not really!

Zeitfracht Medien GmbH
Ferdinand-Jühlke-Straße 7
99095 Erfurt, Deutschland
produktsicherheit@kolibri360.de